THE MINDFUL WEALTH

Using Mindfulness Techniques to Attract Abundance and Happiness.

STANLEY H. PREUSSER

CONTENTS

ACKNOWLEDGEMENTS

I extend my heartfelt gratitude to the readers of "The Mindful Wealth." Your curiosity and dedication to personal growth inspire me. To my family, friends, mentors, and teachers, thank you for your unwavering support. To the publishing team, editors, and designers, your expertise and belief in this work have been invaluable. Lastly, I thank the universe for the flow of inspiration. May the wisdom within guide you on your journey to abundance and fulfillment.

INTRODUCTION

Adopting a Mindful Wealth Mindset

Welcome to a journey that goes beyond the traditional concepts of wealth. In this book, we embark on a transformative exploration of the Mindful Wealth mindset—a path that leads to financial abundance, personal fulfillment, and a profound connection with the world around us.

Imagine a life where wealth is not just measured by the balance in your bank account but by the richness you experience in every aspect of your existence. It's a life where you radiate prosperity, not just for your own benefit, but for the betterment of others as well. This is the essence of the Mindful Wealth mindset.

But what exactly does it mean to embrace this mindset? It starts with a shift in perspective—a recognition that wealth goes beyond mere material possessions. It's about understanding that true abundance encompasses financial prosperity, emotional well-being, meaningful relationships, and a deep sense of purpose.

Embracing the Mindful Wealth mindset means stepping away from the never-ending pursuit of more, and instead, cultivating gratitude for what we already have. It means recognizing that our thoughts and beliefs shape our reality, and by adopting a positive and empowering mindset, we can manifest wealth in all its forms.

One of the key pillars of the Mindful Wealth mindset is conscious awareness. It involves becoming fully present in each moment, engaging with our financial decisions mindfully, and aligning our actions with our values. By doing so, we break free from the autopilot mode of living, where money controls us, and instead, we become the architects of our financial destiny.

In this book, we will explore practical techniques to cultivate mindfulness in our financial lives. We will delve into the power of self-reflection, meditation, and visualization, all of which help us uncover and transform any limiting beliefs that may be holding us back from true abundance.

Moreover, we will dive into the realm of conscious consumption—a realm where we make intentional choices about how we spend our money, ensuring that our financial decisions align with our values and contribute to our overall well-being. We will learn how to prioritize experiences over possessions, and how to invest our resources in things that truly bring us joy and fulfillment.

So, are you ready to embark on a transformative journey towards Mindful Wealth? Buckle up, because this is not just a path of financial prosperity, but a path of personal growth, self-discovery, and making a positive impact on the world around us. Embrace the Mindful Wealth mindset, and prepare to unlock a new dimension of wealth—a wealth that transcends the boundaries of money and touches every corner of your existence.

PART 1

CULTIVATING THE FOUNDATION

"Building a solid foundation is the key to creating lasting wealth and success." - **Unknown**

"Success is not built overnight; it is the result of a solid foundation laid brick by brick." - **Unknown**

"A strong foundation is the cornerstone of sustainable growth and prosperity." - **Unknown**

"A solid foundation provides stability and resilience in the face of challenges on the path to wealth."
- **Unknown**

"To reach new heights of success, one must first focus on building a solid foundation rooted in mindful wealth principles." - **Unknown**

CHAPTER ONE

THE BENEFITS OF MINDFULNESS IN CREATING WEALTH

There is a critical need for an alternative strategy—one that incorporates mindfulness into the process of wealth creation—in a society where the quest of riches frequently becomes associated with stress, competitiveness, and anxiety. The transformational power of mindfulness and how it may overhaul your path to financial plenty are also topics covered in this chapter.

At its foundation, mindfulness is about connecting with life's experiences without judgment or attachment while being completely present in the moment. Something remarkable occurs when we apply this method to the area of wealth building. We develop a sensitivity to the nuances of our financial choices, uncovering information and opportunities that would not have previously occurred to us.

In the middle of our fast-paced, consumer-driven world, we frequently discover ourselves operating on autopilot and making rash financial decisions without taking the long-term effects into account. This tendency is broken by mindfulness, which invites us to take a moment, breathe, and consider the underlying causes of our financial actions.

We get a more acute awareness of our relationship with money through practicing mindfulness. We become aware of our spending patterns, saving behaviors, and wealth-related mindsets. We understand how our thoughts and feelings affect our financial health, which enables us to liberate ourselves from self-defeating ideas and actions.

Being mindful enables us to make deliberate and knowledgeable financial decisions. It urges us to step back from cultural constraints and outside influences so that we may match our financial objectives with our true values. Instead of aimlessly chasing the fantasy of monetary achievement, we start to concentrate on what matters to us most.

Additionally, mindfulness gives us the grace and resiliency to handle the inevitable ups and downs of our financial path. We may address financial losses with calm and clarity rather than being paralyzed by them. We come to understand that genuine riches goes much beyond our material goods, and we learn to separate our self-worth from our financial worth.

Using mindfulness to create wealth creates space for creativity and innovation as well. We access our innate knowledge and open up fresh viewpoints as we learn to live in the moment. We come upon chances that were previously obscured by the cacophony of our hectic life. When we are mentally clear, we may take risky, calculated actions that move us closer to our financial objectives.

We will explore useful methods for integrating mindfulness into your process of wealth development in this chapter. We will look at techniques for developing a mindful relationship with money as well as mindfulness meditation and visualization exercises. By practicing mindfulness, you may access a well of inner knowledge that can change not only your financial situation but also the way you live.

Are you prepared to use mindfulness to your advantage while you pursue wealth creation? Get ready to start a journey that will take you far beyond the boundaries of conventional ideas of wealth and lead you to a place of self-discovery, empowerment, and financial plenty. Let mindfulness serve as your compass while you travel the path to material success and satisfaction.

APPLICABLE TECHNIQUES FOR INCLUDING MINDFULNESS IN YOUR PATH TO WEALTH CREATION

Until today, we were unaware of the transforming potential of mindfulness in generating wealth. Let's now look at some useful tips for incorporating mindfulness into your financial path. You may access a higher level of abundance and fulfillment via mindfulness meditation, visualization exercises, and techniques for developing a conscious relationship with money.

- **Mindfulness Meditation**

Developing awareness and presence via mindfulness meditation is a fundamental discipline. Allocate a certain period of time each day to sit motionless and objectively notice your thoughts, feelings, and sensations. You may learn to notice your financial events without getting caught up in them by engaging in mindfulness meditation. You may make decisions that are in line with your beliefs and long-term goals thanks to this insight.

The cornerstone for increasing awareness in many areas of life, including wealth generation, is the practice of mindfulness meditation. It entails deliberately concentrating your attention in the current moment while dispassionately monitoring your thoughts, feelings, and bodily sensations.

Find a place that is calm and distraction-free where you may sit or lie down to practice mindfulness meditation. Here are some starting points:

- **Settle into a Calm and Comfortable Position**

Put yourself in a calm yet attentive stance by finding a posture that works for you. If sitting cross-legged on a cushion or in a chair with your feet flat on the ground is more comfortable for you, you can also try lying down.

- **Bring your Attention to your Breath**

Gently shut your eyes or avert your sight to focus on your breath. Start by taking a few long, deep breaths to unwind your body and mind. After that, concentrate on your breathing. Without attempting to alter it in any way, simply pay attention to the sensation of the breath entering and exiting your body. Every time you inhale or exhale, be totally present.

- **Observe your Thoughts and Emotions**

As you keep your attention on your breath, ideas and emotions may come to mind. Pay attention to these. Just watch them without judging them, don't get caught up in them. As an objective observer, see yourself accepting all thoughts and feelings as they arise and fade, letting them flow through your consciousness like clouds in the sky.

- **Cultivate Non Judgmental Awareness**

Develop a nonjudgmental awareness by gently bringing your attention back to the present now whenever you detect your thoughts straying from your breathing. Recognize that it's normal for the mind to wander, and treat yourself with kindness and patience. Don't assign a positive or negative name to any moment; instead, learn to accept it as it is.

- **Increase your Awareness**

After getting comfortable with the practice of monitoring your breath, you might decide to increase your awareness of other bodily sensations, external noises, or even your thoughts and feelings. The idea is to continue to be aware of whatever emerges in the present moment with kindness and without judgment.

- **Continue Practicing**

Regular practice is essential to reaping the full rewards of mindfulness meditation. Even if it's just a short period of time, try to set out a definite time each day for practicing. You could gradually lengthen your sessions as you continue to practice.

In addition to fostering peace and clarity, mindfulness meditation improves your capacity to pay attention to your thoughts and feelings related to money. You may become more aware of your monetary habits and beliefs by routinely doing this, which will enable you to make more informed and empowered decisions as you embark on your wealth development path.

Keep in mind that mindfulness meditation is a personal practice, and each individual may have a different experience. Be kind to yourself, curious, and open-minded as you approach the exercise. You will eventually come to understand the tremendous effects that mindfulness meditation may have on both your relationship with money and your general well-being.

- **Exercises in Visualization**

Visualization is an effective strategy for achieving your financial goals. Spend a few minutes each day picturing the perfect state of your finances. Imagine attaining your objectives, enjoying wealth, and being financially free. Use all of your senses and let the feelings and sensations brought on by your vision consume you. By repeatedly seeing the results you want, you develop a mental map that directs your activities and draws possibilities to make your vision a reality.

Exercises in visualization are effective methods for realizing your financial ambitions. You may access the creative power of your mind and connect your thoughts and emotions with the abundance you want to attract by using your imagination and creating vivid mental images of your desired results. Here are some guidelines for conducting visualization exercises:

- **Set a Clear Objective**

Clarify your financial aim first. It may be reaching a specific revenue level, launching a prosperous business, or obtaining financial freedom. Define the specifics of what you wish to materialize, being as exact as you can.

- **Find a Quiet Area**

Decide on a peaceful location where you won't be bothered. It might be a calm area of your house, a tranquil area of nature, or any location that makes you feel at ease and concentrated.

- **Relax your Body and Mind**

Taking a few deep breaths can help you to calm your thoughts and relax your body. Create a tranquil and open state of being inside of yourself by letting go of whatever tension or stress you may be hanging onto.

- **Make a Mental Picture**

Close your eyes and start picturing the desired financial result. Assume that it has already occurred. To make the vision more realistic and vivid, use all of your senses. Imagine the specifics of your ideal financial reality, hear the noises, feel the sensations, and even smell it.

- **Embrace your Emotions**

As you picture, connect with the feelings you will have after achieving your objective. Experience the happiness, appreciation, and contentment that come with achieving your financial goals. Let these feelings of joy enter every cell of your body.

- **Increase your Vision**

Increase the intensity of your imagery to make the exercise more effective. Consider the beneficial consequences your financial achievement will have on your life and the lives of individuals in your immediate vicinity. Watch as prosperity and possibilities come into your life naturally.

- **Regular Practice**

Regular practice is essential for effective visualization exercises. Set aside a specific period of time every day to carry out this activity. Over time, even a little period of concentrated visualization can have a big impact. The impression you leave on your subconscious mind becomes stronger the more times you perform the activity.

- **Take Inspired Action**

Visualization by itself is not sufficient; it requires inspired action as well. Set concrete objectives, make a strategy, and move forward with your financial aspirations using the energy and clarity you receive from the vision. Trust your gut feeling and go in the direction of your vision by taking coordinated action.

Keep in mind that visualization is a creative process and that each person's experience may be different. Allow all doubts or restrictions to be suspended as you fully immerse yourself in the image. Put your faith in the universe and the power of your thoughts to make your financial dreams a reality.

You may connect your ideas, feelings, and behaviors with your intended financial results by consistently doing visualization exercises. Your financial aspirations begin to materialize as a result of this perfect alignment, which also invites possibilities. A successful and plentiful financial reality may be created by using the power of vision.

- **How to Develop a Mindful connection with Money**

Developing a mindful connection with money is becoming cognizant of your monetary behaviors and perspectives. Start by considering your financial principles. Are they empowering or limiting? Any unproductive beliefs should be challenged and replaced with ones that promote success and plenty. No matter how much or how little you have, learn to be grateful for what you do have. Instead of continuously seeking future money, adopt an attitude of sufficiency and learn to enjoy the present.

What emotions do the words "money" or "investments" evoke in you? Anxious, concerned, perplexed, or even ecstatic. Thinking about your investments and financial situation might elicit a wide range of feelings. Everyone experiences these feelings because of the significance of money in our life, whether we like it or not, whether they are professionals in the field or laypeople.

While we have no influence over the direction the market takes or the pay rise we receive at year-end, we do have some control over how we see and plan for our money. Plans for finances and savings are essential for long-term success and financial security. Working with a Certified Financial Planner can help you understand how to accomplish your financial and more important life objectives, such as retiring at age 55 or buying a second home. Making a financial plan can also provide you advice on how to invest your money. Even with a solid financial strategy and a portfolio of assets suited to it, it may be quite challenging to stay grounded in our day-to-day lives. This is particularly true when unfavorable news and market volatility are present. So how can one manage their life and money while maintaining composure? The Buddhist discipline of mindfulness provides a wonderful lens for comprehending and embracing the feelings that arise when we think about our finances.

Being mindful simply means acknowledging and embracing the thoughts, feelings, and emotions you are having at any given time. You might consider the underlying causes of your emotions by objectively acknowledging the feelings you are experiencing. Where and why did it start to grow inside of you? You have the chance to adopt a fresh viewpoint on the problem when you know where your emotions are coming from. With a new viewpoint, you may escape from your previously unpleasant feelings because you will realize that your present viewpoint is backed by careful, focused thinking.

One can feel eager or nervous about swiftly gaining riches, for instance, after hearing about other people's profitable bitcoin investments. That person could realize that these feelings are a result of desiring long-term financial security in the very near future after observing this and giving it some thought. That person could then realize that for the great majority of people, achieving long-term financial stability often requires investing two-thirds of a lifetime. Realizing this helps to relieve restlessness and worry because relatively few people have amassed long-term financial security in a short amount of time.

Creating a conscious awareness of your monetary decisions, attitudes, and actions is the first step in cultivating a mindful relationship with money. It entails using mindfulness to bring balance, appreciation, and harmony with your values into your financial dealings. Once more, let me to provide you with some succinct tips for developing a conscious relationship with money:

- **Consider Your Beliefs**

Consider your financial views as a starting point. Are they restricting or empowering? Are they predicated on plenty or scarcity? Become conscious of any unfavorable or constricting ideas you may have and examine them. Affirmations that promote wealth, success, and a positive connection with money should be used in their stead.

- **Practice Gratitude**

Develop a spirit of thanksgiving for all of your financial resources, no matter how little. Spend some time every day being grateful for the possibilities and financial resources you now have. Focus on what you already have rather than what you lack to cultivate a sense of wealth and satisfaction. Having gratitude allows additional blessings to enter your life.

- **Align with Your Values**

Think about how your values relate to the choices you make with your money. Make sure your money is going toward the things that are most important to you in life. Conscious spending is making deliberate decisions that are consistent with your beliefs, whether that means spending money on memorable events, contributing to worthwhile causes, or setting aside money for the future.

- **Exercise Mindful Spending**

Think twice before making a purchase and consider if it is in line with your values and long-term financial objectives. Take into account the item's or experience's genuine value to your life, which goes beyond simple pleasure. Practice mindful consumerism by staying away from impulsive purchases and concentrating on deliberate, purposeful spending. Choose experiences that promote value above quantity and give lasting fulfillment.

- **Embrace Simplicity and Minimalism**

Explore the idea of simplicity and minimalism in your financial life by embracing them. Clear up the clutter in your physical environment and get rid of everything that is no longer essential. The urge to acquire financial riches is lessened by simplifying your lifestyle, which enables you to concentrate on the things that are actually meaningful and joyful to you. Redirect your resources to activities and investments that are consistent with your ideals and enjoy the freedom that comes with doing so.

- **Practice Conscious Saving and Investing**

Develop a thoughtful approach to saving and investing by practicing conscious saving and investing. Create a plan to routinely save money and establish clear financial goals. Consider saving as a self-care and financial empowerment practice. Explore mindful investment alternatives that are consistent with your beliefs as you amass funds, such as impact investing or socially responsible investing. Make wise choices that advance the greater good and your financial success.

- **Separate Self-Worth from Wealth**

Keep your financial situation apart from how you feel about yourself. Keep in mind that you are more than just your professional accomplishments. Develop self-compassion and recognize your successes that are intrinsic to you and unrelated to money. Accept that your value is not based on your money account and embrace a positive self-image that is unrelated to success in business.

- **Adopt Financial Mindfulness Techniques**

Apply financial mindfulness techniques to your regular financial operations. Approach these chores with concentrated attention and presence, whether you're balancing your budget, going through your spending, or keeping track of your investments. Practice non-judgmental awareness while you pay attention to the feelings and thoughts that surface throughout financial activities. You may improve your financial management skills by practicing mindfulness in these circumstances.

You may move from a state of mindless consumption to one of conscious awareness and empowerment by developing a thoughtful relationship with money. You develop a better awareness of your financial choices, match your behavior with your principles, and infuse your financial life with a feeling of harmony and thankfulness. Discover the transformational power of mindfulness in your relationship with money and embrace the path of mindfulness. You may handle situations or market occurrences that could otherwise lead you to respond negatively by being aware of your emotions, reflecting on them, and reevaluating the issue.

Though it might be difficult, maintaining a conscious outlook throughout life can be quite beneficial, especially when considering your money. I challenge you to adopt a conscious mindset the next time the market is volatile and to take solace in the fact that your investments and money are in order. There is no better time than the present to begin developing a financial plan and investing strategy if this aspect of your life needs improvement.

SPENDING AND SAVING WITH AWARENESS

In a society where consumer items are widely available and constantly advertised, it's simple to engage in mindless buying. Contrarily, mindful spending is an intentional method of managing your money that enables you to make decisions that are in line with your beliefs and financial objectives.

Making a meaningful link between your spending and your financial ideals is what mindful spending is all about, not pinching pennies and scrounging every last dollar. It's important to comprehend how each financial action affects your entire financial situation.

The adaptability of mindful spending is its strength. It doesn't limit you; instead, it gives you the freedom to choose things that make you happy and that work toward your financial objectives. Spending with intention helps you avoid needless debt, accumulate savings, and make progress toward financial security.

Understanding your income and costs, identifying your financial objectives and beliefs, and making deliberate spending decisions are the three pillars of mindful spending.

- **Monitor Your Earnings and Expenses**

Start by being aware of where and how your money is spent. To keep track of your earnings and spending, use a budgeting tool or a straightforward spreadsheet. You'll have a comprehensive image of your financial status after completing this stage, which will also show you where you can cut back on your expenditures.

- **Choose Your Financial Values and Goals**

What financial goals do you have? It can involve paying off debt, setting aside money for retirement, purchasing a home, or contributing to your child's education. Your spending choices will be guided by identifying these objectives and realizing what you value most in terms of money.

- **Make Conscious Spending Decisions**

Start making deliberate purchases whenever you have a firm grasp on your financial situation and your objectives. Check to see if a purchase fits with your beliefs and financial goals before buying one. If it doesn't, decide if the expenditure is required or if you can live without it.

- **Look for Longevity and Quality**

Put quality over quantity as a priority while making purchases. Select goods and services that are dependable, environmentally friendly, and consistent with your values. Spending with intention entails making purchases that will last a long time and eliminate the need for frequent replacements.

- **Put needs above wants**

Make a distinction between your requirements and wants before making a buy. Consider whether the thing or event is necessary for your wellbeing or is just a passing fancy. Before spending on discretionary items, use judgment and concentrate on meeting your true needs.

- **Embrace Minimalism**

A minimalist outlook may tremendously aid with responsible spending. Declutter your physical area and lessen the collection of unneeded belongings to simplify your life. Adopting minimalism causes you to put more emphasis on experiences, connections, and personal development than on material stuff.

- **Practice thankfulness for Abundance**

Develop thankfulness for the resources and money you have at your disposal. Focus on plenty instead of scarcity by recognising and loving what you currently have. An attitude of gratitude encourages satisfaction and lessens the need to continuously seek approval from others by engaging in extravagant spending.

THE IMPACT OF CONSCIOUS SPENDING

Consistently engaging in mindful spending can significantly improve your financial situation. You may attain financial independence and lessen your financial stress by increasing your savings. Additionally, it promotes a better relationship with money, transforming it from an anxiety-inducing factor into a resource for attaining your goals in life.

Spending with awareness is more than simply a financial tactic; it's a way of life that may improve one's financial situation and entire sense of well-being. Decide on your goals, understand your budget, and begin making more thoughtful purchasing selections. Spending with awareness is the first step toward financial wellness.

In Warren Buffet's insightful comments, "Spend what is left over after spending, not what is left over after saving." Making that mental adjustment, giving saving and investing the highest priority, and making sure our spending is in line with our values and financial objectives are all part of mindful spending. Making every rupee work for us in this way would help us realize our goal of achieving financial security and independence.

Spending with awareness and in alignment with your beliefs and financial objectives is known as mindful spending. It entails keeping tabs on your earnings and outgoing costs, determining your financial objectives and core principles, and exercising financial restraint. Spending with intention may lessen financial strain, boost savings, and promote a better relationship with money.

Pay close attention to your spending and saving patterns. Before making a purchase, think about how it will fit with your principles and long-term financial goals. Consider the true value it brings to your life outside the immediate gratification. Avoid making impulsive purchases and instead focus on planning your expenditures. Similar to this, be conscious of your spending and continuously set aside a portion of your income for your stability and future growth.

Creating a thoughtful relationship with money presents a number of difficult problems, one of which is separating your self-worth from your economic worth. Realize that your worth as a person goes well beyond your professional success. Celebrate your intrinsic successes and traits that are unconnected to money, and embrace self-compassion. You may liberate yourself from the stresses and concerns that can obstruct your path to wealth building by divorcing your feeling of self-worth from your financial situation.

Include mindfulness in your financial decision-making by following this advice. Take the time to pause, ponder, and take into account all pertinent variables while making decisions about investments, career options, or company endeavors. Trust your inner knowledge and pay attention to your instincts. Instead of being simply motivated by short-term rewards or societal expectations, make decisions that are in line with your beliefs, passions, and long-term goals.

Keep in mind that practicing mindfulness while you pursue wealth development is a lifelong endeavor. Be kind and gentle with yourself as you master these abilities. Establishing a schedule that enables you to routinely practice these mindfulness practices is important since consistency is vital. Your connection with money will profoundly change over time, enabling you to attract more wealth, financial independence, and general wellbeing.

As you go out on this road of mindful wealth creation, be in the now, have faith in your inner guidance, and let mindfulness serve as your compass.

CHAPTER TWO

OVERCOMING SCARCITY MINDSET: EXPOSING LIMITING BELIEFS

Our limiting beliefs are concealed, like buried treasure, deep inside the recesses of our thoughts. These ideas serve as imperceptible handcuffs that prevent us from reaching our full potential and living an abundant life. The idea that there is never enough for everyone is one of these beliefs that frequently holds us captive. But don't worry! It's time to begin out on a voyage of self-discovery to break free from the scarcity mindset and these restricting ideas.

Picture a day to day existence consumed by monetary battle, where dreams wilt and trust blurs. This is the brutal reality for those caught in the stifling grasp of restricting convictions. These treacherous contemplations fold over our souls like spiked metal, incurring profound torment and sustaining a pattern of hopelessness. Allow us to dig into the tragic outcomes of these convictions, uncovering the profundity of their effect on our abundance process.

In the first place, envision the constant internal torture that goes with restricting convictions. They murmur in our ears, letting us know we are not sufficiently brilliant, adequately gifted, or meriting to the point of making monetary progress. Their words reverberation to us, planting seeds of self-uncertainty and self destructive behavior. We end up incapacitated, unfit to break liberated from the chains of cynicism that tight spot us.

The profound cost of restricting convictions is faltering. They work on our confidence, leaving us feeling disgraceful and inconsequential. We convey the heaviness of steady examination, estimating our value against other people who appear to amass abundance easily. The aggravation of feeling deficient worries our spirits, disintegrating our certainty and lessening our confidence in our own true capacity.

Limiting ideas feed a sense of pessimism when we're at our lowest. We accept a life of financial hardship because we are sure that no matter how hard we strive, we will never be able to change our situation. The aspirations we once cherished become a distant memory, being replaced by a resigning acceptance of mediocrity. Unrealized potential causes us ongoing emotional sorrow.

But things don't stop there. Limiting ideas have negative effects on our interactions and relationships with others.

We become defensive and reluctant to express our aspirations for fear of criticism or contempt. We turn away from individuals who inspire us and choose to be with people who support our limiting views, which keeps us trapped in a destructive loop.

The emotional suffering gets worse with time. We see chances pass us by while secretly understanding that we are the ones preventing ourselves from taking advantage of them. As we think back on the times when we gave into fear rather than pursuing financial plenty, regret becomes our constant companion and a heavy burden we bear.

Limiting beliefs have effects that go beyond our personal lives and influence the way we make financial decisions. We accept positions and vocations that limit our interests and fall short of the material benefits we yearn for. We shrivel from proceeding with potentially dangerous courses of action, persuaded that disappointment is inescapable. Our ledgers lessen, and the feeling of dread toward never having enough immerses us, leaving us deadened in a condition of unending shortage.

Nonetheless, in the midst of the close to home torment and depression, there is a good omen. We have the ability to break liberated from this stifling grasp. It starts with recognizing the overwhelming results of our restricting convictions and gathering the boldness to challenge them. We should overcome our most profound feelings of trepidation and frailties head-on, stripping back the layers of self-uncertainty to reveal our actual potential.

Take a minute to picture yourself standing at the brink of a big ocean. The richness that awaits us is symbolized by the waves smashing against the coast. But our perspective of scarcity says to us, "There isn't enough to go around. You need to hold onto what you have and stockpile it. It's time to disprove that notion and immerse ourselves in the riches all around us.

The first step in removing our limiting ideas is being self-aware. Think for a moment about your beliefs and behaviors towards wealth, success, and abundance. Do you hold views that are based on scarcity or abundance? Do you worry a lot about losing out or not having enough? It's time to bring these unconscious ideas into conscious consciousness by shedding light on them.

It's time to confront your limiting ideas after you've discovered them. Start by examining the evidence for these views. Are they derived from one's own experiences or passed down from ancestors? We frequently acquire views without questioning their veracity. We make room for fresh options and viewpoints by challenging their tenets.

Challenge your scarcity thinking and adopt an abundant mindset in its stead. Change your attention from what you lack to what you have and what is feasible. No matter how tiny, embrace appreciation for the blessings in your life. Celebrate other people's accomplishments and acknowledge that your own success is not diminished by theirs in order to cultivate an attitude of abundance.

It's essential to exercise self-compassion if you want to get rid of a scarcity perspective. Recognize that these ideas were probably created as a means of self-defense or as a result of previous events. Let go of self-criticism and adopt a development and learning perspective. As you proceed on this road of transformation, have patience with yourself.

Find a supportive group of people who have an abundant attitude and who share your beliefs. Participate in discussions that are uplifting and motivating, where accomplishment is acknowledged and shared. Collaborate with others who have already overcome the scarcity mindset, learn from them, and allow their achievements serve as an example for your own development.

Think of living the life you want, free from the restrictions of scarcity. Imagine entering a world where there are abundant chances at every turn. Accept the notion that there is ample opportunity for everyone to experience happiness, success, and prosperity.

Finally, act with inspiration. Consistent work and a desire to stretch yourself are necessary to overcome a scarcity mindset. Set worthwhile objectives that are consistent with your abundant philosophy, then take baby efforts toward realizing them every day. Along the journey, acknowledge your accomplishments and keep in mind that each step you take is a success in and of itself.

Getting rid of limiting thoughts and getting over the scarcity mindset is a path that calls for bravery and introspection. Accept this trip as a chance for personal development and transformation. By letting go of the scarcity mentality, you let in an abundance that is waiting for you. It's time to change the course of your life, take back control, and live a life of limitless potential. Your decision is yours. Let your real potential shine by plunging into the ocean of riches.

We recover our self-worth and reestablish our self-confidence with each stride toward emancipation. We live in a community that is encouraging and empowering to us. We recast our self-talk by substituting empowering affirmations for unfavorable ideas. Even in the face of uncertainty, we take courageous decisions because we are aware that real progress is only beyond our current comfort level.

It takes transformation to release oneself from the agonizing effects of limiting ideas. Resilience, perseverance, and unshakeable self-belief are necessary. The difficulty of questioning our ideas and pursuing an abundant life is greatly outweighed by the suffering of continuing to be mired in a cycle of misery.

So let's find our inner fortitude, let go of our limiting ideas, and start along the road to financial freedom. Even if the emotional suffering was severe, there is enormous joy and fulfillment waiting for us on the other side. It's time to change the course of our narrative, reclaim our authority, and welcome the prosperity and plenty we rightfully deserve.

DOUGLAS UNFULFILLED DREAM

I want to close this chapter with the terrible tale of Douglas, who, like all of us, yearned for a better life but was never able to realize it.

Douglas lived in the little hamlet of Willowbrook, and his life served as a terrible example of the influence of limiting ideas and the scarcity mindset. Douglas was raised in an environment of deprivation and financial struggle. The persistent anxiety of his struggling parents left a lasting mark on his receptive mind.

As Douglas got older, his circumstances appeared to solidify his convictions that success and fortune were out of reach for those like him. His thoughts were closely held by the scarcity mindset, which constantly reminded him that there was never enough for everyone and that the life he desired was only a dream.

The road towards maturity for Douglas was accompanied by these confining ideas. He ached for stability in his finances, daydreaming of a life of prosperity, comfort, and the capacity to support his family. But every time he ventured to move toward transformation, his inner demons attacked him ruthlessly.

The emotional toll of Douglas's struggle was immeasurable. Days turned into weeks, weeks into months, and months into years, but his financial situation remained stagnant. The pain of unfulfilled dreams gnawed at his soul, creating an ache that permeated every aspect of his existence. His spirit withered as he witnessed others around him achieving success, while he felt trapped in a perpetual cycle of scarcity.

Limiting beliefs echoed through Douglas's mind like a never-ending symphony of despair. They convinced him that he was not smart enough, not talented enough, and not deserving enough to break free from the chains of his circumstances. With each passing day, his confidence crumbled, and the spark of hope dimmed, suffocated by the weight of his own self-doubt.

The consequences of Douglas's limiting beliefs reverberated throughout his life. Relationships strained under the burden of financial stress, as he was unable to provide the stability and security he longed to offer. He watched his loved ones suffer, feeling a sense of guilt and helplessness, as his own dreams remained unfulfilled.

The scarcity mindset enveloped Douglas like a suffocating fog, distorting his perception of the world. It colored his every decision, causing him to shrink from opportunities that held the potential for growth and prosperity. He clung tightly to what little he had, afraid to take risks or invest in himself, convinced that he would always be on the losing end of life's battles.

As the years wore on, Douglas's spirit grew weary. The pain of his unfulfilled potential weighed heavily upon him, filling his heart with regret and bitterness. The dreams that once burned brightly within him now flickered like dying embers, a cruel reminder of the life that could have been.

The tragic truth was that Douglas never saw the end of his financial struggle. He never experienced the joy of financial freedom, nor the relief of knowing that his loved ones would be taken care of. His limiting beliefs and scarcity mindset kept him trapped in a cycle of despair, forever separated from the life he so desperately desired.

The story of Douglas serves as a poignant reminder of the devastating impact of limiting beliefs and scarcity mindset. It illustrates the immense pain and despair that can accompany a life overshadowed by self-doubt and a lack mentality. But it also serves as a call to action, a plea to break free from these invisible chains and rewrite our narratives.

May Douglas's story serve as a rallying cry for all those who find themselves caught in the grips of limiting beliefs and scarcity mindset. May it inspire us to confront our fears, challenge our beliefs, and take bold steps towards a life of abundance and fulfillment. Let us not allow our dreams to wither away like Douglas's, but instead, let us rise above the pain and reclaim our power to create the lives we truly deserve.

CHAPTER THREE

DEVELOPING A GROWTH MINDSET FOR ABUNDANCE

Embracing a growth mindset is like awakening a dormant force within us, setting free the limitless potential that lies untapped. It is a paradigm shift that empowers us to see setbacks as opportunities for growth and to view failures as stepping stones on the path to success. With a growth mindset, we understand that our abilities are not fixed, but rather malleable and expandable with effort and determination.

The journey towards developing a growth mindset begins with self-awareness. We must examine our beliefs and thought patterns, identifying any fixed mindsets that may be holding us back. Are there areas in our lives where we believe our abilities are set in stone, where we shy away from challenges or fear making mistakes? Recognizing these limitations is the first step towards dismantling them.

Next, we cultivate a mindset of possibility. We train our minds to see opportunities in every situation, even in the face of adversity. We understand that failure is not an endpoint, but a valuable feedback mechanism that guides us towards improvement. We embrace challenges as gateways to growth and approach them with enthusiasm, knowing that our efforts will lead to personal and financial expansion.

An essential aspect of developing a growth mindset for abundance is nurturing a love for learning. We become lifelong students, hungry for knowledge and eager to acquire new skills. We seek out mentors and role models who embody the growth mindset, drawing inspiration from their journeys and applying their wisdom to our own lives.

In the realm of abundance, collaboration and cooperation thrive. We recognize the power of synergy, where the whole becomes greater than the sum of its parts. By cultivating a growth mindset, we open ourselves to the idea of collaboration, celebrating the achievements of others and seeing their success as a testament to the possibilities that await us all.

Challenges become opportunities for growth. We no longer shy away from them, but rather embrace them with open arms, knowing that they are stepping stones on our path to abundance. We develop resilience and perseverance, understanding that setbacks do not define us, but rather serve as fuel for our determination to succeed.

As we develop a growth mindset for abundance, we let go of the fear of failure and step into the realm of possibility. We become the architects of our own destinies, empowered to create a life of prosperity and fulfillment. Our mindset becomes a magnet, attracting opportunities, connections, and resources that align with our desires and ambitions.

Release the limitations of fixed thinking and embrace the boundless potential within you. As you nurture your minds with positivity, curiosity, and resilience, we unlock the doors to a life of abundance, where dreams become realities and the possibilities are truly infinite.

LETTING GO OF FEAR

Fear has a way of holding us hostage, keeping us confined within the boundaries of our comfort zones and preventing us from embracing the abundant possibilities that await us. But what if we could break free from fear's grip and step into a life filled with abundance, joy, and fulfillment? Let us embark on a transformative journey of letting go of fear and embracing the limitless potential that lies within us.

Fear is a natural response, a primal instinct designed to protect us from perceived threats. It whispers in our ears, cautioning us against taking risks and urging us to stay within the confines of familiarity. It convinces us that the unknown is a treacherous territory, one that should be avoided at all costs.

But what if we were to reframe our perception of fear? What if we were to see it not as a barrier, but as a catalyst for growth? For within every fear lies an opportunity—a chance to expand our horizons, to push beyond our limitations, and to discover new depths of courage and resilience.

To let go of fear, we must first acknowledge its presence. We must confront our fears head-on, understanding that they are often based on assumptions and past experiences rather than objective reality. By shining a light on our fears, we strip them of their power and open ourselves up to the possibility of transformation.

Next, we cultivate a mindset of trust and faith. We trust in ourselves, in our abilities, and in the support of the universe. We understand that fear is not an indicator of danger, but rather a signpost pointing towards growth and expansion. With trust as our guide, we can navigate the unknown with a sense of curiosity and excitement, rather than trepidation.

Letting go of fear also requires a shift in perspective. Instead of focusing on potential failure or negative outcomes, we choose to focus on the possibilities and opportunities that lie beyond fear's grip. We reframe fear as a stepping stone towards growth, understanding that even if things don't go as planned, we will learn valuable lessons and gain newfound strength and resilience.

Courage becomes our ally on this journey. We recognize that courage is not the absence of fear, but rather the willingness to take action in spite of fear. It is through courageous action that we expand our comfort zones, shatter limiting beliefs, and create space for abundance to flow into our lives.

To let go of fear, we must also surround ourselves with a supportive community. We seek out like-minded individuals who uplift and encourage us on our journey. We share our fears and vulnerabilities, knowing that in doing so, we not only release their hold on us but also inspire others to do the same.

As we release fear's grip, we step into a world of infinite possibilities. We embrace abundance in all its forms— financial abundance, abundance of love and relationships, abundance of opportunities, and abundance of joy and fulfillment. We recognize that the universe is abundant, and as children of the universe, we are deserving of that abundance.

So, let us embark on this liberating journey of letting go of fear. Let us break free from the chains that bind us and step boldly into the unknown. For it is in that space of uncertainty and vulnerability that we discover our true potential and unlock the doors to a life filled with abundance, growth, and immeasurable joy.

EMBRACE THE POWER OF SYNERGY

In a world that often celebrates individual achievement and self-reliance, we may overlook the extraordinary power that lies in synergy—the coming together of diverse minds, talents, and energies. Synergy is the alchemy of collaboration, where the whole becomes greater than the sum of its parts. It is through embracing the power of synergy that we unlock a pathway to abundance and unparalleled success.

Imagine a group of individuals with unique perspectives, skills, and experiences, united by a common vision. Each person brings their own strengths to the table, complementing and enhancing one another. As they collaborate and pool their resources, ideas flow freely, innovation flourishes, and obstacles are overcome with greater ease.

When we embrace the power of synergy, we recognize that success is not a solitary journey, but a collective endeavor. We understand that by joining forces with others, we can amplify our impact and achieve far more than we ever could on our own. Synergy allows us to tap into a vast reservoir of knowledge, talents, and connections, propelling us towards abundance in ways we could never achieve in isolation.

Synergy brings forth the magic of shared creativity. As we collaborate with others, ideas spark and intertwine, birthing innovative solutions and groundbreaking ventures. The combined wisdom and diverse perspectives of a synergistic team generate fresh insights and open doors to untapped opportunities. In this realm of collaboration, limitations dissolve, and breakthroughs become the norm.

But synergy is more than just a means to an end; it is a transformative process that enriches our lives on a personal level. Through collaboration, we learn from one another, expanding our horizons and challenging our preconceived notions. We discover new facets of our own abilities and uncover hidden talents as we contribute to the collective effort.

In the realm of synergy, trust and respect are the pillars that uphold the collaborative spirit. We recognize that each person brings value to the table and that every voice deserves to be heard. We cultivate an environment where diverse opinions are welcomed and conflicts are seen as opportunities for growth and deeper understanding. By embracing the power of synergy, we foster a sense of unity and harmony that propels us towards abundance.

Collaboration isn't without its difficulties. It requires compelling correspondence, undivided attention, and a readiness to relinquish inner self for everyone's best interests. It requires a profound feeling of compassion and the capacity to fabricate solid, steady connections in light of trust and shared values. However, the compensations far offset the endeavors, as we witness the outstanding development and satisfaction that emerge from cooperative undertakings.

In the domain of development and overflow, collaboration turns into a core value. We search out associations and joint efforts that line up with our vision and values. We sustain an organization of similar people who share our goals and are focused on inspiring each other. Together, we make an aggregate power that pushes us towards our common objectives and extends our ability for overflow.

Embrace the force of collaboration. Break liberated from the thought that achievement is a lone pursuit and perceive the groundbreaking expected that lies in coordinated effort. By meeting up, pooling our assets, and commending the novel commitments of every person, we release a power that rises above your singular impediments and makes ready for overflow to stream into your life and the existences of others.

THE POWER IN SELF AWARENESS

In the profundities of the human experience, there exists a significant misfortune — a misfortune of living without really knowing ourselves. It is an excursion tormented by disarray, botched open doors, and a determined sensation of being lost in the shadows. The shortfall of mindfulness projects a foreboding shadow over our lives, leaving us helpless against the excruciating outcomes that emerge from an absence of understanding and association with our actual selves.

Envision a day to day existence lived on autopilot, floating capriciously through the flows of presence without a compass to direct us. We stagger as the days progressed, disengaged from our longings, interests, and reason. The fantasies that once consumed splendidly inside us currently seethe behind the scenes, choked by the heaviness of similarity and cultural assumptions.

Without mindfulness, we become detainees of our own oblivious examples and restricting convictions. We rehash similar mix-ups, uninformed about the decisions that lead us down reckless ways. We damage our connections, disrupting our opportunities for certified association and closeness. We pursue outside approval, looking for satisfaction in the endorsement of others as opposed to sustaining our own valid selves.

The outcomes of self-ignorance are broad and significant. We wind up caught in poisonous connections, rehashing disastrous examples that leave us injured and broken. We settle for short of what we merit, tolerating unremarkableness in our vocations and individual lives since we neglect to perceive our actual worth. We numb our torment with interruptions, suffocating our inward voices in thoughtless utilization, addictions, and interruptions that just develop the void inside.

The absence of mindfulness denies us of our power — the ability to settle on cognizant decisions, the ability to make a daily existence lined up with our most profound longings, and the ability to show our fantasies into the real world. We become simple onlookers in our own lives, watching potential open doors cruise us by, realizing where it counts that we are prepared to do a great deal more, however unfit to break liberated from the chains that tight spot us.

The aggravation of self-ignorance isn't restricted to our singular lives; it saturates our collaborations with others and our general surroundings. We unintentionally hurt those we love, uninformed about the effect of our words and activities. We add to the propagation of cultural shameful acts, ignorant concerning the manners by which our own predispositions and molding shape our convictions and ways of behaving. We exist in a condition of disengagement, unfit to manufacture significant associations with others since we have not associated with ourselves.

In the most profound openings of our being lies a wellspring of undiscovered possibility, standing by without complaining for the second when we stir to our actual selves. It is through self awareness that we open the doorway to a development mentality and the overflow that looks for us. Self consciousness is the impetus that lights our excursion of individual change, pushing us towards a day to day existence loaded up with development, flexibility, and boundless potential outcomes.

Envision an existence where difficulties are not detours, but rather venturing stones. Where difficulties are not viewed as disappointments, however as any open doors for learning and development. Such a world is inside our range, and it starts with developing mindfulness — the profound knowing about what our identity is, our assets, shortcomings, convictions, and examples.

Self awareness is the foundation of a development mentality — the conviction that our capacities can be created and worked on through devotion, exertion, and a readiness to learn. It is through this awareness that we perceive our own true capacity for development and embrace the conviction that our knowledge, gifts, and abilities are not fixed elements, but rather moldable and expandable.

With self awareness, we become sharp eyewitnesses of our viewpoints, feelings, and ways of behaving. We notice oneself restricting convictions that keep us down — the voice of self-question that murmurs in our ears, asking us to leave nothing to chance and stay away from gambles. By being conscious of ourselves, we gain the ability to challenge these convictions, supplanting them with enabling accounts that fuel our development and push us towards overflow.

Self awareness permits us to distinguish and beat our usual ranges of familiarity — the natural domains that keep us stale and keep us from arriving at our maximum capacity. It is through awareness of self that we perceive when we are keeping ourselves down, sticking to the recognizable as opposed to embracing the unexplored world. With conscious of self, we push past our constraints, embracing uneasiness as an essential venturing stone on the way to development and overflow.

As we develop our self awareness, we develop a significant feeling of interest and receptiveness. We approach difficulties and disappointments with a development situated mentality, seeing them not as obstructions, but rather as any open doors for learning and personal growth. We comprehend that misfortunes are not impressions of our value, but rather simple diversions on the excursion towards our fantasies.

Our intrinsic resilience—the capacity to overcome adversity, endure in the face of challenges, and adapt to change—is unlocked by self-awareness. The ability to manage the problems of life with elegance and persistence comes from self-awareness. We understand that in order to progress, we must put out effort, be persistent, and be prepared to accept discomfort as we push ourselves above our comfort levels.

Failures are not seen as a point of no return with a development mentality, but rather as instructive experiences that help us succeed in the future. We accept setbacks as chances for development and learning since we know they are only temporary. We view problems as stepping stones towards personal and professional progress rather than becoming discouraged by them.

We may liberate ourselves from the constraints of self-doubt and constrained thinking by adopting a growth mentality. No matter where we start, we think we can learn, adapt, and get better. We view challenges as merely barriers that can be surmounted with tenacity and grit.

By adopting a growth mentality, we understand that our potential is not fixed but rather able to be expanded. We actively look for chances to advance our skills and flourish. Knowing that it is an effective instrument for progress, we welcome comments. We appreciate other people's accomplishments because we are aware that they serve as a reminder of our own potential.

We can unleash our creativity and ingenuity when we adopt a growth mentality. We are not constrained by conventional norms or previous assumptions. Instead, we investigate novel ideas and push the limits of what is understood. To achieve development and plenty, we are willing to venture outside of our comfort zones and take calculated risks.

People around us are inspired and uplifted when we demonstrate a development mentality. Our positivity and faith in the ability of progress spread. We exhort people to see their own potential and relentlessly pursue their goals.

It's not always simple to cultivate a growth attitude for plenty. It necessitates introspection, tenacity, and a readiness to face and dispel our own limiting ideas. But the benefits are incalculable. By developing a growth mentality, we may realize our full potential and live fulfilling, prosperous, and joyful lives.

When plenty counts, a growth mentality serves as our compass, pointing us in the direction of boundless opportunities and riches. When we have firm faith in our ability, we take control of our own future and design a life that is bursting with happiness, fulfillment, and numerous rewards. Let's grab the bull by the horns in a world where dreams come true, resiliency thrives, and the universe works in our favor as we embrace the transforming power of a growth mindset. Ensure that you are developing

PART 2

MASTERING FINANCIAL AWARENESS

"Financial awareness is the key that unlocks the door to financial freedom. Master it, and you hold the power to shape your destiny." – **Unknown**

"Embrace the power of financial awareness, for it is the cornerstone of wealth creation and the pathway to a life of abundance." – **Unknown**

"In the realm of financial success, knowledge is power, but awareness is liberation. Master your financial awareness, and watch your dreams soar." – **Unknown**

"Financial awareness is not just about numbers and calculations; it is about understanding the language of money and making informed decisions that align with your goals." – **Unknown**

"Become the master of your financial destiny by cultivating unwavering awareness. With every informed choice you make, you shape a brighter and more prosperous future." - **Unknown**

CHAPTER FOUR

MINDFUL MONEY MANAGEMENT: BUDGETING AND SAVING STRATEGIES

It's all too simple to get caught up in the swirl of financial concerns in the busy turmoil of our contemporary lives without stopping to consider the effects of our choices. The outcome? A journey paved with lost chances, growing debt, and a strong sense of being disconnected from our full financial potential. We pay a price for poor money management that extends far beyond the figures on a balance sheet and permeates into the very fabric of our lives, leaving a path of suffering and regret in its wake.

Imagine living in a world where every salary disappears before our eyes, leaving us struggling to survive. We feel the weight of financial worry pressing down on us, which disrupts our sleep and strains our relationships. We are unable to escape the chains of financial instability and are stuck in a never-ending cycle of living paycheck to paycheck. As the pressing needs of daily life take precedence, our dreams are left to collect dust on shelves that are often empty.

Lack of financial awareness may send us down a dangerous path of reckless spending, debt entrapment, and living above our means. The attraction of rapid enjoyment blinds us to the long-term repercussions of our choices, seducing us. We build up debt through credit cards, loans, and other financial commitments that hover over us like foreboding storm clouds and continuously throw a shadow over our goals and objectives.

Beyond our bank accounts, poor money management has far-reaching negative impacts. It damages our mental health and undermines our sense of worth and self-worth. As we look at the mess we've made, we experience a strong sensation of remorse and humiliation. We become caught in a loop of critical self-talk, berating ourselves for our perceived shortcomings and lack of self-control. Our emotions are burdened by the burden of financial mismanagement, which drains our resources and robs us of the happiness and freedom we deserve.

Even in relationships, poor money management may put even the strongest ties under stress. Conflict and anger grow as a result of financial stress. Arguments break out over petty issues like excessive spending, unpaid bills, or conflicting financial objectives. The once-firm basis of trust breaks down, creating a landscape of unfulfilled promises and shattered dreams.

We cannot undervalue the toll that is taken on our mental health. Our peace of mind is constantly being eaten away by worry, anxiety, and restless nights. Bills, debt, and other financial commitments take up much of our mental space, leaving little room for creativity, joy, or pursuing our hobbies. The financial responsibilities we unintentionally established entrap us and prevent us from embracing the countless opportunities life has to offer.

But there is hope despite this depressing reality. The suffering that results from poor money management serves as a wake-up call and a motivator for reform. It forces us to examine ourselves and face our personal financial issues. It ignites a strong yearning for an alternative future—one where we are in charge of our financial future, and awareness and intention serve as our guides while making decisions.

We liberate ourselves from the bonds that bound us by incorporating mindfulness into the way we handle our finances. We set out on a quest of financial and personal empowerment. We take control of our financial future by consciously choosing decisions that are consistent with our beliefs and objectives. We grow to be profoundly appreciative of the resources at our disposal, finding satisfaction in simplicity and careful financial management. We develop a sense of happiness that transcends worldly belongings when we learn to differentiate between our necessities and desires.

We recover our power—the capacity to design a life of financial security, wealth, and fulfillment—through conscious money management. We foster fortitude and discipline, and a fresh sense of direction. For our aspirations to develop and materialize, we lay a strong foundation.

So, let the discomfort and unfavorable consequences of not practicing money management awareness serve as a trigger for change. They should inspire us to start along a new road of financial understanding, empowerment, and abundance. By adopting mindfulness in our financial management, we open the door to a life where our financial well-being coincides with our greatest desires—a life where joy, contentment, and the freedom to live honestly take the place of anguish and regret.

CONSCIOUS CONSUMPTION

Conscious consumption arises as a defiant act of self-expression and empowerment in a society where materialism rules supremely, where advertising bombard us at every step, and where the quest of material items frequently obscures our genuine beliefs. It is a call to action to break free from the mindless rush of consuming and match our spending with our core beliefs, paving the road for a more purposeful and deliberate life.

Imagine living in a society where every dollar we spend counts as a vote for the kind of society we want to live in—one that values social justice, sustainability, and human connection. As we carefully evaluate the effects of our purchases on the environment and the welfare of others, conscious consumerism enables us to become engaged members of our community and our own sense of fulfillment.

The act of thoughtful judgment is at the core of conscious consumption. It encourages us to take a moment to reflect before making a purchase and to reflect on our ideals. Does it accurately reflect who I am and what I believe in? Does it advance my general well-being as well as the welfare of others? By intentionally directing our expenditures, we recover the ability to control our own narratives and the environment.

Conscious consumption includes not just the material goods we purchase but also the experiences we decide to spend money on. We learn the backstories of the brands we believe in, looking for businesses that follow moral standards, support charitable organizations, and place a priority on sustainability. Knowing that our money is helping a bigger cause when we support local companies, small shops, and community-driven projects, we enjoy doing so.

A certain amount of introspection and self-reflection are necessary in order to match our expenditures with our ideals. It causes us to reevaluate what it really means to have a really fulfilled life and to challenge conventional conventions and expectations. It teaches us to discern between our needs and our wants, realizing that genuine wealth is found in the richness of our relationships, experiences, and contributions to the world rather than the accumulation of material goods.

Conscious purchasing is a transforming path that pushes us to discover joy in simplicity and release ourselves from the cycle of mindless consumerism. It encourages us to practice the art of conscious living, in which we relish the present, express our thanks for what we have, and look to experiences rather than material things for fulfillment. We learn that seeking significance and purpose rather than worldly items might satisfy the gap within of us.

Through this dance of mindful consumerism, we rediscover our agency and reimagine how we interact with money. Our value is now determined by the influence we have on the world and the principles we uphold, not by the stuff we own. By accepting our individual path and recognizing the beauty of authenticity, we free ourselves from the constraints of comparison and social expectations.

BUDGETING

Budgeting serves as a light of hope—a lifeline that directs us towards a future of financial stability and empowerment—in the busy chaos of our modern lives, when the pull of instant satisfaction tugs at our wallets and thoughtless spending threatens to destroy our financial goals. It is a straightforward but powerful technique that has the potential to open up a world of opportunities, to liberate oneself from debt, and to set off on a path towards one's biggest aspirations.

Think of the weight that is lifted off your shoulders when you finally take charge of your financial future. You will feel a sense of release that will revive your spirit and rekindle your interests. A passport to a life where your hard-earned money acts as a catalyst for prosperity, stability, and progress, budgeting is the key that opens this door.

Budgeting is really a dance—a complex choreography of income and spending, wants and requirements, aspirations and reality. It's a fine line that calls on us to develop astute financial observational skills, to confront our biases, and to make deliberate decisions that are consistent with our core principles.

Start by taking a few deep breaths, bringing your awareness to the present, and imagining the life you want. What are your monetary objectives? What dreams long to be fulfilled? Let's begin the path of budgeting with a clear aim in mind and a set of straightforward yet effective tactics that will help us reshape our financial landscapes.

Simple techniques emerge as rays of hope as you make your way through the maze of budgeting, pointing you in the direction of financial security. The first tactic is the art of classification, which is the art of classifying your spending into different groups. Every component in your budget, from food and leisure to housing and transportation, is a chapter in your financial memoir. You may make your spending more understandable and make sure that your finances are in line with your objectives by giving each area a budget.

The magic of tracking, which involves keeping a close eye on every dollar that enters and leaves your life, should then be embraced. By practicing mindfulness, you may get insight into your spending habits, spot areas where you might want to make improvements, and acknowledge your accomplishments as you go. With tracking, you take control of each chapter of your financial story, rewriting it with a specific aim.

Budgeting, though, is about more than simply restraint; it's also about balance and self-care. Set aside a chunk of your money for indulgence and joy so that you can enjoy the small things that make you happy without feeling guilty. It may be a regular date night, a weekend trip, or a fresh book that captures your interest. Keep in mind that creating a budget is not about deprivation; rather, it is about finding harmony in your financial decisions and matching your spending to your ideals.

And remember the value of flexibility and resilience when difficulties emerge and unforeseen costs threaten to ruin your well-planned budget. Because life may be unpredictable, your budget should be flexible. Create an emergency fund so that you have a safety net to lean on during times of ambiguity and peace of mind. Recognize that your budget is a live, breathing thing that changes along with you and alter it as necessary.

Celebrate all of your successes, large and little. Your dedication and tenacity are demonstrated by every dollar saved, every debt forgiven, and every objective accomplished. Give yourself a moment of appreciation and a pat on the back for your accomplishments. Allow these occasions to motivate you by serving as a reminder of the influence that budgeting has on improving your financial situation.

But creating a budget involves more than just limiting ourselves or spending less on the things we enjoy; it also entails building an abundant mentality and making decisions that really please us. Examine your spending carefully and distinguish between requirements and wants. Set a goal for yourself to cut back or eliminate spending on things that don't support your moral principles so that you have more money for experiences, connections, and personal development.

As you start your budgeting path, keep in mind that success is not always a straight line and that obstacles could appear. Find a method to accept them as chances for development, education, and path correction. Keep your composure in the face of difficulties by remembering that every step you take, no matter how tiny, will bring you closer to financial independence.

Budgeting is not a solitary activity; it flourishes in the supportive environment of a community. Assemble a group of like-minded people who are committed to achieving your financial goals around you.

The approach could appear difficult at first since it demands addressing your financial realities head-on. It entails evaluating your income and expenses, examining the depths of your spending patterns, and admitting both your accomplishments and your failings.

You can experience some aggravation as you face the unpleasant realities about your needless spending, impulsive purchases, and mounting debt. But keep in mind that this journey is not about condemnation or humiliation; rather, it is about development, change, and finally, emancipation.

Keep in mind that budgeting is a lifelong habit as you negotiate the emotional terrain of the process. It necessitates perseverance, commitment, and a desire to advance. Accept the road with open arms because it is there that you will learn the independence, empowerment, and joy that come with controlling your financial future.

Infuse your budgeting journey with intention, purpose, and unshakeable commitment by letting your heart lead the way. Accept the feelings that come up because they will help you go forward. And keep in mind that you are not alone while you navigate the waters of financial stability. Countless others stand beside you, sharing the same hopes, dreams, and struggles.

ALIGNING SPENDING WITH VALUE

In a world where the allure of consumerism pulls us in countless directions, aligning our spending with our values becomes an act of rebellious creativity—a dance of conscious choices that transcend the ordinary and breathe life into our deepest convictions.

Imagine stepping into a vibrant marketplace where each stall represents a different aspect of your values—a kaleidoscope of colors, scents, and textures that reflect the tapestry of your beliefs. The first stall beckons with sustainable clothing, crafted from ethically sourced materials, adorned with intricate designs that celebrate the beauty of slow fashion. As you run your fingers over the fabrics, you feel the stories woven within each thread—the hands that labored with love and care, the communities uplifted through fair trade practices.

A little café hidden within a grove of trees is only a few yards away, and the scent of freshly made coffee draws you there. The beans are carefully chosen from farms that practice environmental responsibility and are expertly roasted to maintain their distinctive characteristics. You can taste the dedication to quality and respect for nature with every sip. A symphony of tastes dances on your tongue, arousing your senses and serving as a constant reminder of the connection between your enjoyment and the health of the earth.

Further along, you come to a studio where expert hands fashion beautiful ceramics out of clay. The artist talks about her skill and her ambition to produce beautiful things with a small environmental impact. Every item exudes authenticity and individuality—a physical representation of uniqueness that goes beyond the mass-produced and speaks to your spirit.

You discover that you are drawn to events that feed your spirit as you stroll around this marketplace of values. The potential to provide a helping hand, to elevate people in need, and to contribute to a more equal society beckons when one volunteers at a neighborhood community center. You see the effect of your efforts during these times of service and come to understand that impact, rather than possessions, is the actual measure of riches.

You learn that it's not only about the things you buy and the experiences you have—it's also about the tales they represent—as you engage in this creative dance of spending in accordance with your principles. Every purchase you make turns becomes an intentional act, a deliberate stroke on the canvas of your life. You take pleasure in searching out organizations and projects that share your values, in supporting them, and in joining a broader movement for good.

You develop a stronger relationship with yourself and a profound awareness of what matters to you most via this creative alignment. Your financial decisions become an extension of who you are and a visible representation of your principles. Knowing that even the smallest purchase has the potential to have a significant impact on industries and encourage other people to take similar actions, you embrace the ability to change the world via your consumption.

So, let your spending turn into a piece of art—a masterwork produced with intention. Pick colors that respect ecology, fairness, and compassion when painting with a cause. Create a future that is in line with your most ardent beliefs. And may you discover contentment, purpose, and a deep feeling of connection—to yourself, to others, and to the planet we share—in this artistic tapestry of coordinated spending.

Spending in accordance with your principles is a transforming journey that calls for careful consideration and deliberate action. To help you on the road to matching your spending with your beliefs, consider the following concrete steps:

- **Choose Your Core Values**

Spend some time considering and defining your basic principles. What is most important to you? Is it social justice, community involvement, environmental sustainability, or individual well-being? List your values and order them according to their importance in your life.

- **Analyze Your Present Spending Patterns**

Consider your recent purchasing habits and evaluate how well they adhere to your ideals. Check your purchases, subscriptions, and debt obligations. Do you believe your spending in any areas goes against your morals? Note these alignment errors.

- **Educate Yourself**

Increase your knowledge of how consumer decisions affect the topics that concern you. Investigate the policies and principles of various corporations, organizations, and brands. Look for certifications, initiatives to have a social effect, and ethical sourcing. Make educated judgments by being informed.

- **Establish Your Priorities**

Based on your values, choose the areas where you wish to concentrate your expenditures. Is it buying eco-friendly items, promoting social causes, or patronizing small local businesses? Establish a clear vision for your spending priorities.

- **Establish Budgetary Boundaries**

Create a budget that is consistent with your beliefs. Set aside a certain amount of money for the things that matter most to you. This will enable you to make deliberate decisions within your limits and prevent overpaying.

- **Practice Mindful Decision-Making**

This can be done by pausing and asking yourself a few important questions before to making a purchase. Do these things reflect my values? Is it required? Does it advance my general well-being as well as the welfare of others? Consume mindfully, keeping in mind how your decisions will affect you over the long run.

- **Research and Support Ethical Brands**

Look for brands and businesses that share your beliefs and conduct research on them. Look for businesses who place a high priority on social responsibility, fair trade, sustainability, and ethical labor practices. Support companies that are dedicated to changing the world for the better.

- **Reduce, Reuse, Recycle**

Adopt a sustainable and mindful minimalist approach. Reuse products wherever feasible, cut out on needless purchases, and recycle properly. Spend your money on long-lasting items and prioritize quality over quantity.

- **Giving Back**

Spend some of your money on neighborhood projects or charity organizations that share your ideals. Encourage groups that strive to improve society and the environment. Small donations may have a big impact when they are used for worthwhile causes.

- **Reflect and Make Adjustments**

Consistently evaluate your financial decisions and consider if they are consistent with your growing ideals. Adapt your strategy as necessary, making deliberate changes to maintain congruence between your spending and your beliefs.

Keep in mind that matching your spending to your beliefs is a continuous effort. It calls for self-awareness, thoughtfulness, and a readiness to make decisions that are consistent with your own values. By embarking on this path, you may develop a deeper and more purposeful connection with your money, so bringing about good change in both your life and the world.

MINDFUL DEBT MANAGEMENT

Few tasks are as oppressive and difficult as carrying unmanaged debt amid the huge sea of financial challenges. It is a situation that has the potential to dominate our thoughts, throw a shadow over our lives, and make us feel as though we are caught in a never-ending cycle of anxiety and sorrow. Lack of attentive debt management has a negative impact on our emotional health as well as our financial health, straining our relationships and robbing us of our peace of mind.

Life has become a significant hardship for many individuals. A persistent reminder of the debt that looms enormous and casts a long shadow on their hopes and dreams hangs over your head every day as you wake up. Their ability to completely enjoy life's potential is taken away by the voice of debt that drowns out the joy of the present. It undermines their feeling of self-worth and stalks you like a persistent ghost in your thoughts.

Debts accumulate along with the restless nights and anxiety that gnaws at your very core. Every bill that shows up in the mailbox is like a stabbing to the heart, a stinging reminder of mounting debt. You are bound by the weight of the past, stifling all hope for a better tomorrow.

Relationships may suffer from poor debt management, which puts a tremendous amount of stress on the people we care about. Money turns into a quiet battleground where hatred grows unrestrained like a plant and tension simmers under the surface. A chasm that threatens to swallow the love and connection that previously flourished is created when the joy of shared experiences is eclipsed by the ongoing concern about money.

On the other hand, emancipation starts with a mental shift—a brave choice to face the truth of your financial circumstances and your debts. Mindful debt management is a path toward empowerment and self-discovery rather than a fast fix or miraculous cure.

Recognizing the suffering and anxiety that debt has caused in your life is the first step, but you must resist letting it define you. It involves taking a deep breath, gathering the courage to face the facts, realizing your financial duties, and setting out on a path to financial freedom.

A dedication to take charge of your finances and making informed decisions is mindful debt management. It entails carefully monitoring your expenditure, separating needs from wants, and coordinating it with your actual priorities. It necessitates self-control, sacrifice, and a readiness to forgo short-term pleasure in favor of long-term financial security.

But a greater transformation—a release of the spirit—lies beyond the concrete measures. An chance to develop resilience and a profound sense of your worth beyond material possessions is presented by mindful debt management. It's an opportunity to define success on your own terms and put experiences and connections before things.

A burden is removed from your shoulders with every debt payment you make, marking your progress and demonstrating your perseverance. You gain tenacity and tenacity that will benefit you in all facets of life as you travel the occasionally hazardous and twisting road of debt repayment.

Although the path to conscious debt management is not simple, it is one that is worthwhile. It is a way to recover your financial independence, get your peace of mind back, and lay the groundwork for a bright future. With bravery and conviction, embrace this trip, understanding that each stride forward is also a step away.

A SIMPLE AND CREATIVE DEBT MANAGEMENT PATTERN WITH MINDFULNESS

Practicing mindful debt management becomes an art in the world of personal finance, where debts might seem like ruthless creatures lurking in the shadows—a beautiful ballet of self-awareness, self-control, and unflinching resolve. We must accept our weaknesses, face our financial realities head-on, and take back control of our financial destinies on this trip.

Imagine entering a vivid theater where you are the star of the show as a valiant protagonist giving a magnificent performance. You start the first act by reflecting on yourself and going in-depth about your connection with money. Spend a time acknowledging the feelings of dread, humiliation, and aggravation that come up when you think about your obligations. Accept them since they are the foundational elements from which resilience is created.

It's time to choreograph the dance of conscious debt management now that you have self-awareness at your disposal. Make a thorough inventory of your debts as a physical representation of the monetary loads that are dragging you down. This is the first gracious step. List all of your debts along with their amounts, APRs, and required minimum payments. This acknowledgement should fuel your will to overcome them.

The rhythm of strict budgeting takes center stage as the music builds. Create a sensible budget that balances your income and spending. As you plan your expenditures, channel your inner conductor to make sure that every note is in tune with your financial objectives. Look for ways to reduce wasteful spending so you may use the money saved to reduce your debt.

In the middle of this financial symphony, it's crucial to have a strong network of supporters who will encourage you, give you advice, and give you a shoulder to cry on when things go tough. Reach out to family members, friends, or support groups that can offer priceless guidance and inspiration during your debt management journey.

But attentive debt management goes beyond pragmatism; it also emphasizes finding comfort in self-care activities. Imagine yourself in the midst of the mayhem engaging in peaceful pursuits that feed your spirit. Contribute energy outside taking expanded walks, lowering yourself in an enrapturing book, or tidying up. These little seasons of loosening up revive your soul and build up your will to go for it.

Celebrate even the little accomplishments as you follow your commitment the board strategy reliably. show respect for yourself on the additional responsibility you make, the premium you save, and the creating size of your in the event account. These achievements show that your tenacious exertion and affirmation are paying off; they are the crescendos in your symphony.

In any case, there could moreover be times when you feel like your show is in danger of being obscured by exhaustion. You can experience questions that push you to return to past spending models or forsake your commitment repayment plan completely. This is an optimal chance to channel your inside champion — the one driven by an internal compass, diligence, and decided trust in your own power. Manage these tangles straightforwardly and recall the best honor you can achieve: an everyday presence freed from commitment.

Imagine the last endeavor as the curtains close: a triumphant, liberating, and financially freeing end. Feel the weightlessness in your soul when each responsibility is paid off and a weight is disposed of. This open door will allow you to pursue wants, handle prospects, and embrace a future freed from commitment.

You accept three unmistakable parts in the heavenly weaving of aware commitment the leaders: guide, craftsman, and onlooker. Go on this excursion with energy, imaginativeness, and unflinching assurance. Let care and point be your helpers for every action you do, including money related decisions. Recall that you are following after some admirable people as you turn through the beautiful developments of commitment the board. You are circled by a troupe of various performers who are on similar courses and who are pulling out all the stops consonant result.

So bow, my commitment champion, since you have started a historic way that goes past money and into the genuine focus of what your character is. With each cognizant action, you recuperate your power, change your money related story, and clear the path for a future where accomplishment and abundance rule unique.

Discerning money the leaders fills in as the chief in the gathering of individual spending plan, sorting out the delightful equilibrium among arranging and saving procedures. A solid instrument empowers us to manage our money related destinies and centers us toward a plentiful and prosperous future.

Recognize a wellspring of motivation as we approach another financial time: a call to put the data secured to use and change it into noticeable outcomes. This present time is the best opportunity to apply the illustrations of cautious money the chiefs to your everyday daily practice and prepare for financial abundance and opportunity.

Sincerely vow to make monetary arrangements that are reliable with yourself, to our objectives, and to your convictions. Face each challenge to assess your spending, discard your wasteful penchants, and put your money into projects that will fulfill you, help you with creating, and make you feel fulfilled.

Despite how little you save, truly focus on it. Regardless, when it's inconvenient or alluring to spend your money indiscreetly, be wary about saving some of it. Review that every dollar saved is a piece closer to a possible destiny of freedom from a futile daily existence and sufficiency.

For the most part central, foster the care seeds that at this point exist inside you. Stay aware of circumspection and cognizance of your financial choices, considering their deliberateness and long stretch effects. Encourage a firm sureness that you have some command over your financial future, move beyond challenges, and continue with a copious presence.

Since real change starts with movement. Understanding the essentials of careful money the board is inadequate; You ought to take on these traits, give them life, and grant them to affect your ordinary financial decisions.

Outfitted with the information, experiences, and approaches we have learned, stroll forward with unfaltering reason. Comprehend the course of savvy cash the board, understanding that with each monetary arrangement you set up, each cost you examine, and each dollar you save, you are getting ready for an unrivaled future for you along with your loved ones.

Opportunity has shown up. You have the power. Take advantage of it and set before off the best approach to financial flourishing, overflow, and the presence you truly merit.

PART 3

CREATING WEALTH-BUILDING HABITS

"Success is not just about making money; it's about creating wealth-building habits that lead to a life of abundance." – **Unknown**

"The journey to financial freedom begins with small but consistent steps. Build wealth-building habits one day at a time, and watch your dreams turn into reality." – **Unknown**

"Your habits determine your financial destiny. Choose wisely and cultivate wealth-building habits that will shape your future." – **Unknown**

"Wealth is not a destination; it's a journey fueled by disciplined habits and unwavering commitment to your financial goals." – **Unknown**

"The key to building wealth lies in the power of your daily habits. Make each day count and let your consistent actions pave the way to financial success." - **Unknown**

CHAPTER FIVE

THE ART OF GOAL SETTING: TURNING DREAMS INTO REALITY

Imagine a ship that is adrift at sea, being buffeted by ferocious seas without a compass to direct it. The crew is worn out and discouraged as they sail aimlessly, their aspirations floating aimlessly in a huge ocean of unrealized potential and squandered possibilities. The misery of a life without direction or purpose is the harsh reality of ignoring the skill of goal planning. This is how many individuals have spent their lives, and many of them have met horrible ends. You don't want to go through that yourself, I'm sure.

We give our aspirations to chance when we disregard the power of goal setting. As the curtains draw on our dreams, we are reduced to mere spectators, staring with wistful regret for what could have been.

Without specific objectives, we become mired in a never-ending cycle of mediocrity. We bumble through life without a sense of direction, like lost souls in a thick fog. Our days pass by in a routine mist, and as time goes on, our inner fire grows less.

Giving up on the skill of goal-setting implies giving in to the appearance of ease. We choose the route with the least amount of difficulty and turn inward to the security of our comfort zones. However, the eerie presence of regret—the unrealized ambitions that silently plead for our attention—lies inside the boundaries of familiarity.

Neglecting goal planning has harmful repercussions on every element of our life. We become victims of our own sloth and captives of circumstance. The aspirations that once blazed inside us now smolder as they are stifled by complacency.

Without objectives, we lack direction and concentration. As a result of pointless diversions and useless activities, our days degenerate into a collection of dispersed pieces. Time escapes us like sand, leaving us with an empty feeling and unrealized potential.

Unrealized dreams are one of the consequences of ignoring the skill of goal planning. When we reflect on our life, we do it with a sad heart, wondering what may have been possible if we had had the guts to aim higher. We are prevented from living the life we were supposed to live by the regret, which weighs on us like an anchor.

You could now be floating there or have visited the area in the past. But to get out of this situation, recover your power, and awaken the hidden dreams within, start by taking care of all the good things you neglected to perform. begins with adopting the skill of goal setting, a transforming process that gives our dreams life and pushes us in the direction of a better future.

Setting goals helps us reclaim control over our life. We take charge of our own destinies and with unflinching tenacity steer ourselves in the direction of our goals. Each objective turns into a ray of hope that leads us through choppy waters and illuminates the way to our full potential.

By ignoring the skill of goal-setting, we deprive ourselves of the chance to advance, change, and improve as individuals. We deprive the world of our special abilities and gifts, leaving a gaping hole where our contributions might have had an impact.

So, my friend, break free from the bonds of negligence and take back control of goal-setting. Give your dreams significance and intention by breathing life into them. You move closer to the life you were meant to live with every goal you make and action you take.

Goal-setting discomfort acts as a reminder and an urgent call to action. Adopt the skill of defining goals to create a route leading to fulfillment. Seize your dreams; they are the compass that will lead you to a life of prosperity and happiness. Time has come. Set sail towards the horizon of potential and build a future beyond your wildest dreams.

INVESTING CONSCIOUSLY

Michael looked out the window of his office with mixed feelings of sadness and yearning. He had been living paycheck to paycheck for years while seeing others enjoy the benefits of good investments. Although he aspired for a life of financial stability and independence, it always appeared to be just out of grasp.

But all that changed one day.

An essay about mindful investment that Michael came across struck a chord with him on a deep level. It talked about making investments that not only increased wealth but also had a beneficial effect on the world. It also talked about matching financial decisions with personal ideals. He felt a spark of promise and optimism kindled by it.

Michael set out on a journey of self-education and development because he was determined to escape his unchanging financial circumstances. He attended seminars and studied books, soaking up all the information he could on mindful investment. He plunged headlong into the world of finance armed with his newly acquired knowledge and a ferocious drive.

Michael soon understood, however, that mindful investing was a very emotional and introspective process and wasn't simply about statistics and charts. It forced him to face the misconceptions and anxieties he had about money, removing the many years' worth of uncertainty and unease.

Michael learned the value of self-awareness as he dove deeper into the realm of investment. When making investing decisions, he learnt to pay attention to his feelings and thoughts to recognize the impact of fear and greed. By engaging in mindfulness exercises, he learned how to stand back, distance himself from irrational impulses, and make decisions that are in line with his long-term objectives.

Michael agreed that doing your homework and using caution was essential. He was aware that attentive investing needed a thorough knowledge of the businesses and markets he chose to participate in. He scrutinized financial records, examined industry trends, and sought for businesses that shared his principles of innovation, sustainability, and social responsibility.

But arguably the greatest life-changing lesson from Michael's tale was the understanding that investing wasn't just a solo activity. It was a chance for him to get in touch with a group of people who believed in conscious wealth creation and shared his enthusiasm for it. He joined investing groups and participated in discussions about the potential of investments to improve the world in ways other than for monetary gain.

Michael's relationship with money underwent a significant transformation as a result of mindful investment. It was now a tool for empowerment and good development rather than a cause of tension and anxiety. He no longer felt like a passive bystander in the world of money; instead, he felt like an active participant who used his capital to back ventures and causes that shared his ideals.

Michael's portfolio steadily increased over the years, showing not just his financial success but also the beliefs and principles that governed his decisions. But it wasn't just about the statistics; it was also about the satisfaction and sense of accomplishment he experienced from realizing the impact his efforts were having.

When Michael looked back on his trip, he saw how mindful investing had completely changed not only his financial circumstances but also his view on life. It had given him a fresh feeling of empowerment, purpose, and optimism. He had not only amassed money via the power of thoughtful investment, but had also contributed to a more just and sustainable society.

Conscious investment emerges as a lighthouse—a guiding light amid the storm—in a world where financial markets fluctuate like a stormy sea. It asks us to take a step back from the craze and adopt a more deliberate and mindful strategy for increasing our wealth.

Beginning with a change in perspective, moving away from the idea of immediate rewards and instant satisfaction, is the first step in mindful investing. It challenges us to dig deeper beyond the surface-level figures and graphs to the values and concepts that underpin our financial choices.

Conscious investment is fundamentally about coordinating our financial decisions with our larger life objectives and beliefs. It forces us to think about the possible rewards on our investments as well as their effects on the environment. It inspires us to make a conscious effort to build a better future by investing in businesses that value sustainability, social responsibility, and ethical business practices.

However, investing with mindfulness involves more than simply picking the appropriate stocks or funds. It's a routine—a method of being in the world of investing. In order to successfully manage the ups and downs of the market, it encourages us to acquire a strong feeling of awareness and present. It teaches us to maintain our composure and to resist the urge to make snap judgments motivated by greed or fear.

Patience, another virtue that is required for mindful investment but is frequently put to the test by market volatility. It serves as a reminder that investing is a long-term activity, more like a marathon than a sprint. It motivates us to maintain our goals in mind, have faith in compound development, and resist the impulse to adjust our plans hastily in response to transient variations.

Risk management is one of the most important components of conscious investing. It recognizes that every investment has some inherent risk, and that a wise investor tries to comprehend and successfully control those risks. It encourages us to diversify our holdings, do in-depth study, and make thoughtful judgments as opposed to acting on the spur of the moment.

Self-reflection, a constant process of learning and improvement, is another aspect of mindful investment. It challenges our presumptions, challenges our prejudices, and encourages us to learn more. It nudges us to look for other viewpoints and maintain an open mind to fresh opportunities. We can improve our financial strategy and make better decisions by being more self-aware.

In the end, mindful investment is a continuing examination of the relationship between money accumulation and ethical behavior. It urges us to take on the role of a responsible steward of our financial assets, to make deliberate investment decisions, and to make a difference in the world.

Michael's tale serves as a potent reminder that investment is about leveraging our financial resources as a force for good, rather than just increasing personal wealth. It involves matching investments to ideals and having a beneficial influence on the world. By investing mindfully, you may break free from the constraints of conventional finance and go on a journey that results in both material prosperity and significant social change.

So, think about adopting mindful investing if you find yourself yearning for financial independence and a deeper sense of purpose. Make it the starting point for a life makeover. As Michael learned, money has the capacity to fuel your aspirations, liberate your decisions, and mold a future that is both affluent and consistent with your core principles.

FINDING FINANCIAL FREEDOM THROUGH BUILDING MANY STREAMS OF INCOME

This exceptional destination—a life where you have the ability to create, the flexibility to pursue your passions, and the stability to do so—can be reached by developing several sources of income. Join me as we go off on this fascinating quest to uncover your inner potential.

Enter the region of possibilities, where limitations imposed by convention no longer apply to you. Creating many sources of income is similar to tending a beautiful garden, where different opportunity seeds are nurtured until they bloom into a symphony of wealth. Each stream represents a different channel via which your abilities, knowledge, and interests might flow, enhancing not just your material well-being but also your spiritual well-being.

The days of surviving exclusively off of a wage are long gone. Instead, you adopt an attitude of growth and look for new revenue sources that are consistent with your goals and principles. Your heart beats faster as you learn about entrepreneurship since this is the field where dreams may come true. You let your creative side run wild and establish companies that represent your special vision and meet the requirements of others. You take control of your own fate by guiding the business ship with unflinching resolve and unshakeable faith in your abilities.

But it goes farther than that. You harness the power of investing to put your money to nonstop work for you. You develop into a shrewd investor who can confidently and intelligently negotiate the volatile financial market. Your investment portfolio transforms into a tapestry of possibilities, with each investment standing for a portion of your financial destiny.

Passions and talents develop into sources of revenue rather than merely hobbies. By using your creativity to its full potential, you may share your talents with the world and experience fulfillment. You learn that your artistic abilities are not merely sources of delight but also prosperous possibilities that contribute to the fabric of your riches, whether you like to express yourself through writing, painting, performance, or any other kind of artistic expression.

You take use of technology's strength and maximize its enormous potential in this digital age. By utilizing the reach of digital media, you may reach a large audience who is eager to learn from you. Your internet presence develops into a source of motivation and influence that draws possibilities and alliances that increase your revenue streams more than you could have ever imagined.

But the goal isn't only to make money. More than merely increasing your money, having various sources of income allows you to live a life of freedom and purpose. It's about having the means and freedom to live your life as you want, to contribute to causes that excite your heart, and to leave a lasting legacy that goes beyond money.

ADDITIONAL SOURCES OF INCOME

Numerous revenue streams beckon in the great field of possibility, each one offering a route to material prosperity and personal fulfillment. Let's imagine a world of opportunities where imagination and ingenuity combine to create a life with boundless potential. We live in a world like that. Imagine a painter who shares their enthusiasm and knowledge with interested pupils by teaching painting workshops in addition to selling their artwork. Their revenue comes from the selling of their works of art as well as the fees they charge for mentoring other people as they pursue their own artistic endeavors. They create a vivid canvas of financial security and creative joy with each brushstroke.

Or consider a digital entrepreneur who creates an online empire with a laptop and infinite inventiveness. They produce engrossing blog entries that not only motivate readers but also bring in money through affiliate marketing and paid content. They create engaging films that entertain while also bringing in money from commercial deals and product endorsements. Their money comes from a variety of digital sources, each of which serves as a tributary to the river of financial independence.

Enter the world of real estate now, when an investor owns a variety of rental properties rather than simply one. Each property serves as a distinct source of revenue for them, and it is derived from the monthly rent they get from renters. They have a network of investments that produce passive income and lay the groundwork for long-term prosperity, so their financial stability is not dependent on a single investment.

Think of a modern-day nomad who sells their talents in a variety of fields: the freelancer. They may be a professional consultant, a gifted writer, or a great graphic designer. Their revenue comes from several clients, with each project denoting a separate stream across their competence and mobility, they move across a variety of businesses, tapping into many sources of revenue to build a stable financial foundation.

Consider the inventor, whose brilliant inventions not only improve people's lives but also bring in money. They have patents on their ideas and license them to businesses in exchange for a cut of the revenues. As creative concepts come to life and appeal to a large audience, royalties provide them with a source of revenue. They create an endless stream of riches with each new invention.

Not to be forgotten is the astute investor who diversifies their holdings by including mutual funds, equities, and bonds. Dividends, capital gains, and interest are the three main sources of their revenue; each investment generates a different stream. They manage the constantly shifting financial market, and their expertise and insight enable them to profit from intelligent investment choices.

These are just a handful of the numerous revenue streams that may be found in this enormous universe of possibility. Each stream indicates a different way to get money and lead an abundant life. Explore your interests, make use of your skills, and embrace innovation as you set off on your own journey. As you weave together many sources of money to create a symphony of financial success, let your imagination be your guide.

Remember that maintaining each line of income with attention and effort is just as important as diversifying your revenue. Your wealth will grow if you receive a consistent stream of income, much like a river does with a continuous flow of water. Be resourceful, brave, and receptive to the limitless opportunities that lie ahead.

The cornerstone of success in the world of money creation is the development of habits. It involves developing a way of living that leads to financial plenty. Let's think about the importance of developing wealth-building habits and the amazing changes they may bring as we wrap up this section of the book.

It takes a certain attitude to develop wealth-building behaviors rather than merely having money. It involves reprogramming our attitudes, convictions, and actions to reflect a prosperous vision. By developing these habits, we take control of our financial future and create opportunities, stability, and fulfillment in our lives.

But keep in mind the strength of constancy. Through consistent repetition, habits are formed. They demand commitment, self-control, and the ability to keep going in the face of difficulties.

So, keep in mind that the adventure starts within as you set out. Make a commitment to yourself, establish definite goals, and surround yourself with encouraging people. Learn from mistakes, accept development, and seek out information.

CONCLUSION

ADOPTING A CONSCIOUS WEALTH LIFESTYLE

Imagine living in a world where wealth is more than just financial data. In this life, abundance is measured not just in terms of financial goods but also in terms of the variety of experiences, relationships, and inner contentment. This is the core of adopting a mindful wealth lifestyle—a journey that leads us on a road of profound transformation and enlightens us on what success really means.

In a society where excess and spending are frequently associated with riches, we find ourselves yearning for something more profound and significant. We desire a life in which our behaviors are consistent with our principles and every financial choice we make represents who we truly are. It involves developing a positive relationship with money—one that is based on awareness, purpose, and intention.

Adopting a mindful wealth lifestyle entails developing a keen awareness of how our decisions affect not just our own lives but also the lives of those around us. It's about realizing how our financial choices affect other people's well-being, the environment, and future generations.

The act of intentional spending is at the core of a mindful wealth lifestyle. It involves changing our emphasis from thoughtless consumption to intelligent investment—investing in experiences that feed our souls, in goods and services that are consistent with our beliefs, and in causes that stoke our enthusiasm for effective change. One purchase at a time, it's about making decisions that have a good impact on the planet.

Importantly, embracing a mindful wealth lifestyle goes beyond spending—it encompasses the way we earn, save, and invest our money. It's about building a financial foundation that is grounded in integrity and purpose. It's about aligning our work with our values, seeking opportunities that allow us to make a meaningful impact, and creating a legacy that extends far beyond our own lifetimes.

Yet, in this quest, we must also acknowledge the emotional aspects of wealth. It's about exploring our relationship with money, unearthing any limiting beliefs or fears that hold us back from experiencing true abundance. It's about embracing a mindset of abundance, gratitude, and generosity—knowing that wealth is not a finite resource but an infinite wellspring that can be shared and multiplied.

A mindful wealth lifestyle is not always simple to adopt. It necessitates reflection, bravery, and a readiness to question conventional norms and expectations. It calls on us to reject the seduction of immediate fulfillment and embrace long-term, sustainable progress. It challenges us to strike a balance between taking pleasure in the here and now and planning for a prosperous and secure future.

Oh, the benefits that await us after this adventure, though! Every financial choice becomes a chance for self-expression and making a good difference, leading to a life of profound joy. It's a way of life where having money doesn't limit you but rather helps you develop yourself, effect change, and cultivate a better world.

Consequently, my friend, I cordially ask you to go out on faith and begin this incredible journey of embracing a conscious wealth lifestyle. When making financial decisions, put your faith in your instincts, listen to your emotions, and practice mindfulness. Accept the satisfaction of mindful purchasing, the force of intentional earning, and the transforming potential of a wealthy attitude.

Let's reinterpret what it means to be really prosperous together. Let's make a world where the depth of our relationships, the influence of our deeds, and the satisfaction of our hearts are used to assess riches instead of merely the size of our money accounts. Adopt a conscious financial lifestyle, and you'll see how your life transforms into a tapestry of prosperity, significance, and limitless opportunity.

FINAL WORDS

As a whole, "The Mindful Wealth" is a transforming path toward a new paradigm of prosperity, meaning, and conscious life. It is a manual that gives you the power to maximize your riches, live a life of meaningful purpose, and match your actions with your ideals.

I want you to think back on the significant lessons and insights you have learned as you read this book's closing chapters. Accept the benefits of mindfulness, deliberate spending, and thoughtful investing. Release your fears of scarcity and your limiting beliefs to embrace the limitless opportunities that lie ahead.

But keep in mind that real change happens in your life, not only on the pages of a book. It happens as a result of your actions and execution. Consequently, I urge you to proceed. Put the concepts and techniques you have learnt to use. Start by making a conscious financial strategy, defining clear targets, and taking tiny, regular steps in the direction of your objectives.

Share your experience with others because when we motivate and encourage one another, positive change spreads quickly. Start talks in your community about mindful wealth, engage in meaningful dialogue about it, and act as a catalyst for a change in people's perceptions of wealth that is more sustainable and mindful.

Additionally, keep in mind that mindful wealth is about having a beneficial influence on the world in addition to your own personal benefit. Look for chances to support causes that align with your values. Encourage groups and projects that advance social and environmental well-being. Make use of your money as a force for good and a driver of progress.

Lastly, never stop developing and learning. Continue learning more about resources, going to workshops, and meeting others who share your goal for a mindful wealth lifestyle. Embrace a network of people who will support you and inspire you while you travel.

As you put this book away, keep in mind that you have the ability to build a life of conscious riches. Believe in your ability to create plenty, live a purposeful life, and affect change. Believe in the power of your aspirations, and allow them lead you to a life that is genuinely prosperous in all ways.

Now, take a time to picture the life you want—a life where riches isn't only defined by financial things, but by the quality of your relationships, your sense of joy, and the good you do for other people. Step into the world of limitless possibilities by embracing the power of conscious riches.

The path to thoughtful wealth-building has begun. Accept it, take care of it, and allow it guide you toward a life of genuine prosperity, fulfillment, and meaning. You possess the ability to generate the money you deserve and want. Time has come. Accept the mindful wealth lifestyle, then go out on your path.